THE GRAPPLE MANUAL

KENDO NAGASAKI

THE PROFESSIONAL WRESTLERS
FOUND WITHIN THIS BOOK
ARE HIGHLY TRAINED ATHLETES.
PLEASE DO NOT IMITATE OR
COPY THEIR ACTIONS.

THE GRAPPLE MANUAL

Heroes & Villains
FROM THE GOLDEN AGE
OF WORLD WRESTLING

WEIDENFELD & NICOLSON

CONTENTS

Hello grapple fans!

I had the great pleasure of introducing televised wrestling to millions of viewers during my time presenting *World of Sport*. With its colourful, larger-than-life characters, extreme athleticism and incredible contests, professional wrestling is one of the most exhilarating entertainment spectacles, attracting a huge following across the globe.

It doesn't matter if you are from Beaver, Utah; Chihuahua, Mexico or Darlington, England, whether your heroes are Big Daddy, Hulk Hogan, Giant Haystacks or 'Exotic' Adrian Street, *The Grapple Manual* showcases the big, bad and bizarre celebrities of world wrestling.

Theatre in the extreme, these men and women go into battle each night of the week, performing death-defying moves, putting their lives on the line all in the name of entertainment for a blood-baying public.

Please remember, though, that all of the wrestlers featured in this book are complete professionals who have undergone years of intense training so please don't attempt anything found within these pages at home, whether it may be imitating their flamboyant fighting moves or wearing a silver jumpsuit or figure-hugging leotard when you clearly haven't got the figure for it.

Dickie Davies

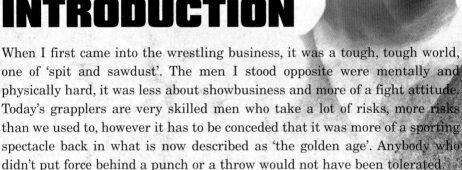

INTRODUCTION

When I first came into the wrestling business, it was a tough, tough world, one of 'spit and sawdust'. The men I stood opposite were mentally and physically hard, it was less about showbusiness and more of a fight attitude. Today's grapplers are very skilled men who take a lot of risks, more risks than we used to, however it has to be conceded that it was more of a sporting spectacle back in what is now described as 'the golden age'. Anybody who didn't put force behind a punch or a throw would not have been tolerated.

My own experience of this rough-house vocation is no better exemplified than the night I unmasked the previously unbeaten Count Bartelli. Bartelli was a hard man and his pride wouldn't have allowed him to be defeated without being beaten to a pulp. When the Count's mask finally came off his nose was badly damaged, his lips swollen and blood was seeping from his ear. It had been an epic battle.

I was fortunate in being able to hold my own, but also had the ability to entertain when it was required. These two attributes underscored my own success in the notoriously harsh and fickle business of professional wrestling.

This book is a celebration of the larger than life characters that make up the extraordinary and wonderful world of wrestling – a profession I am extremely proud and privileged to have been a part of.

Kendo Nagasaki

KENDO NAGASAKI

From his debut in the early 1960s until his final bout in 2001, Kendo Nagasaki dominated the British heavyweight wrestling scene, becoming the greatest masked wrestler of his generation. The masked samurai warrior's origins are shrouded in mystery – but legend has it that he was due to represent his country at Olympic level in wrestling when a life-changing experience led him to live the life of a deceased samurai warrior.

From his very first appearance his aggressive, martial arts wrestling style caused a sensation among followers of professional wrestling. Clearly not one for following the rules, Nagasaki wasted little time in gaining victory over all the popular ring stars of the day. Fans soon became entranced by his piercing red eyes and noticed a missing index finger on his left hand, widely-reported to be the result of a bizarre samurai initiation ceremony.

Nagasaki's most famous early victory came at Stoke, England in 1966 when he ended the 20-year unbeaten run of fellow masked star Count Bartelli – the loser to unmask in public for the first time. The result of the match was reported in wrestling publications around the world and a wrestling legend was born. In a memorable televised bout against 'blue-eye' giant Big Daddy, Kendo's mask was pulled off and for the first time viewers saw the warrior's shaven, tattooed head. Kendo Nagasaki achieved further fame as part of a BBC documentary when he was the subject of world-renowned artist Sir Peter Blake, and the resulting work of art has been displayed in major galleries across the world.

Famed for his 'Kamikaze Crash' signature move – a devastating manoeuvre where he somersaulted onto the canvas whilst carrying his opponent on his back – Nagasaki was voted 'Wrestler of the Millennium' in a UK nationwide poll. In 2001 Kendo Nagasaki competed in his last ever bout, the last victory occurring in Stoke, where he had defeated Count Bartelli 35 years before.

KAMIKAZE CRASH

Kendo Nagasaki is a master of numerous martial arts including Judo, Aikido and Kendo. The influence of such disciplines can clearly be seen in his aggressive grapple style. He is famed for the 'Kamikaze Crash' – a forward-rolling movement which crashes Kendo's full weight onto the ribs and stomach of his opponent – an acrobatic signature move guaranteed to leave the toughest opponents flat on their back.

JAKE 'THE SNAKE' ROBERTS

Jake Roberts has become a legendary figure throughout world wrestling, although not always for the right reasons. The son of wrestler Grizzly Smith, who wrestled for the National Wrestling Alliance in the 1970s, Jake was born Aurelian Smith. His rise to wrestling prominence started in the NWA where he made his debut in 1975. Promoters and fans alike quickly took notice of his devastating DDT finishing move which would become a feature of his matches from then on.

Upon joining the World Wrestling Entertainment (WWE) Jake started to bring a pet snake into the ring with him. Damien, as the snake was called, would sit in a bag by the ring and when Jake had finished off his rival the bag would be opened and Damien would slither all over the terrified opponent.

The ring persona of Jake continued to grow, and the promoters would waste little time in inventing new and sometimes ludicrous ways of introducing Damien into the proceedings. That is until the tragic day when Jake's slippery companion got his comeuppance when super-heavyweight wrestler 'Earthquake' flattened the rasslin' reptile with his unattractively titled 'butt drop' manoeuvre. However, this regrettable incident didn't force Jake into changing his name because it wasn't long before a new pet, named Lucifer, made its debut and the serpent shenanigans started all over again.

Jake made his final appearance for the WWE at Wrestlemania VIII where he was defeated by The Undertaker, before jumping ship heading for rival World Championship Wrestling (WCW). After further grapple success, Roberts made a surprise return to the WWE in 1996 at the Royal Rumble and continued to pummel the opposition. However, it was Jake Roberts' increasing reliance on drugs and alcohol that was his biggest enemy. His problems were further increased when he was prosecuted by authorities claiming animal cruelty after a snake in Jake's possession had apparently been found severely malnourished. Whatever his struggles outside of the ring, at his peak Jake 'The Snake' Roberts deserves a place among wrestling's élite for his powerful and athletic performances against the crème of the profession.

'MAIN MAN'
MARTY JONES

Marty Jones is quite possibly one of the greatest technical wrestlers ever to emerge from England. The Oldham-based mid-heavyweight proved to all comers that he was 'Simply The Best', as his Tina Turner ring entrance music implied. Marty began wrestling when his father took him to an amateur gym following school playground fights due to him being teased because he wore glasses. He soon took to the sport, and amateur wrestling turned to professional when the 'Main Man' was thrown in at the deep end when a promoter needed a last-minute substitute in a contest. Marty stepped in to face Stoke's celebrated lightweight Bobby Ryan and after an admiral performance his new career path was secured with him soon acquiring the nickname of the 'Lancashire Lion'.

During his early days Marty would work at Manchester's meat market by day and wrestle in the evenings. A long-standing feud with fellow Lancastrian Mark 'Rollerball' Rocco provided audiences with some of the most spectacular and violent matches ever seen in UK rings, Marty beating Rocco in 1978 when both wrestlers put their respective championship belts on the line in a 'Winner Takes All' showdown. The animosity grew ever stronger and they were still opposing each other right up until Rocco's retirement 13 years later.

A well-known and popular face in Mexico and Japan, the 'Main Man' counts tagging with André the Giant against Antonio Inoki and Fujinami as the highlight of his 100 world title bout career. Having bowed out of life on the canvas Marty now runs a successful public house in the town of Shaw, Lancashire, England.

'NATURE BOY' RIC FLAIR

His trademark 'Whhoooo!' and debonair style make Ric Flair one of the most respected, charismatic and influential wrestlers of the modern age. Born Richard Fliehr in Memphis, Tennessee, the fledgling Ric Flair was already a high school heavyweight wrestling champion in his teens. He was trained for the professional circuit by legendary American matman Verne Gagne, entering the profession for the AWA promotion in 1972 holding George 'Scrap Iron' Gadaski to a 10-minute draw!

Two years later Flair headed for the NWA Mid-Atlantic area, where the 'Nature Boy' defeated Paul Jones for the Mid-Atlantic Television Title. This began an unparalleled run of ring honours but fate dealt a cruel blow when Flair was involved in a plane crash during October 1975 in which he broke his back in three places. He was told by doctors he would never wrestle again and it is a measure of the tenacity of Ric Flair that a little over 12 months later he was back in the ring and heading for more victories.

Eventually Flair found his way into WCW where he was recognised as the World Heavyweight Champion. His career in the WCW soured when he quit and wound up appearing for the opposing organisation WWE, but with the WCW Heavyweight Belt still adorning his waist. It is reported that because Flair owned the belt the WCW organisation had to buy it back for a whopping $75,000. Flair, now in his late fifties, continues to be one of the busiest wrestlers in the profession, often wrestling six nights a week and in matches that could go to an hour or more. Very much of the old school, Ric Flair has demonstrated that whilst having the gift of the gab, it is skill in the ring that determines the long-term success of a wrestler.

BIG DADDY

Big Daddy is without doubt Britain's most popular heavyweight ever. Christened Shirley Crabtree (Shirley being traditionally a boy's name in the Crabtree family), the big Yorkshireman proved very adept at playing rugby league before the lure of wrestling took a hold, as it had his father before him. In the 1960s Shirley wrestled as 'The Battling Guardsman' due to him having served in the Coldstream Guards for a time, in the process acquiring a version of the British Heavyweight Championship. In the mid-1970s Shirley decided it was time for a change of image and adorned his bulk with colourful leotards and made his entrance to the ring wearing sequinned top hats and gowns tailored for him by his wife Eunice.

His new adopted ring name 'Big Daddy' was taken from a character in Tennessee Williams' play *Cat On A Hot Tin Roof* and having re-invented himself, the popularity of Big Daddy soared to new heights for a wrestler with him being famed for his trademark moves the 'Belly Butt' and the 'Big Daddy Splash', where his full weight landed on an opponent. Big Daddy's battles with Giant Haystacks in tag team and occasionally solo action filled halls around the UK and kept millions glued to their television clashes. EMI Records persuaded Big Daddy to record a version of his entrance music 'We Shall Not Be Moved' which was issued as a single record in 1980. Ill health dogged his later career and he retired from wrestling in 1992. Big Daddy died, aged 67, after suffering a stroke in 1997.

BIG DADDY
SPLASH

The United Kingdom's favourite 'Daddy' used his 24-stone bulk to devastating effect when he squashed his opponents into submission with the 'Big Daddy Splash'. This would more often than not be performed to a crowd's chorus of 'easy, easy, easy' = the wrestler's signature chant.

THE BIG SHOW

At 7' 1" tall The Big Show is just that, one of wrestling's giants. After excelling at college basketball, Paul Wight was soon spotted and offered the opportunity to train at the famous Power Plant gym of WCW. He made his big-time debut in 1995 billed simply as 'The Giant', claiming to be the son of the wrestling legend André the Giant and wanting to avenge his late father by defeating Hulk Hogan. Wight was subsequently defeated and developed an ongoing feud with The Hulkster. The Giant then started a super-heavyweight feud with the 'Loch Ness Monster' – alias Britain's own Giant Haystacks – which would result in a major victory for Wight at Uncensored '96.

Having fought his way to solo and tag championship victories Wight jumped ship and signed a 10-year deal with the rival wrestling organisation WWE in 1999, which resulted in him being renamed 'The Big Show'. The Big Show's celebrated choke-slam aka 'The Showstoppa' – where the goliath lifts his opponents up by the neck and crashes them down onto the canvas – is felt to full effect in contests with the likes of The Rock and The Undertaker. As you can imagine his 35-stone bulk is always used to bone-crushing effect. Today, The Big Show remains the latest in a long line of crowd-pulling wrestling giants.

COUNT BARTELLI

For nearly 20 years Count Bartelli was Britain's most famous masked wrestler and strongman. His career in a hood came to an end in 1966 when he faced fellow masked star Kendo Nagasaki who inflicted Bartelli's first defeat. Not to be deterred Bartelli continued wrestling, this time with his face clearly seen. 'The Count', as he was later known to everyone, had his first professional contest billed as Jeff Condor against the World Flyweight Champion Johnny Summers in Chester in June 1939. Before The Count had a chance to rise to the top of the sport, he was called up to serve in the army during the hostilities of World War II. As luck would have it, his posting to Singapore in 1946 allowed the young Count to further extend his wrestling experience as he staged boxing and wrestling tournaments for the troops posted around the region. He would go on to wrestle professionally in Malaysia where he built up a strong and loyal following.

Upon Bartelli's return to the UK in 1947 promoter Arthur Wright suggested a mask and a change of image, and from there the legend of Count Bartelli was born. Count Bartelli became a huge attraction in the north of England, taking on all comers and successfully retaining the right to wear his trademark facial covering. After the shock defeat by Nagasaki, Bartelli brought back the Commonwealth Heavyweight belt from a tour of Australia, a belt he would keep until his retirement from wrestling in 1986. In his later years Count Bartelli worked tirelessly raising money for charity with his feats of strength and was known to show his softer side by caring for orphaned animals. Count Bartelli died in 1993 aged 70.

THE ROCK

The man for whom the phrase 'rock hard' was invented. 'Know your role and shut your mouth' and 'Layeth the Smacketh Downeth' are just two of his catchphrases as The Rock became the hero for a new generation of wrestling addicts.

Dwayne Johnson was perhaps destined to find his way into the ring. All set for a career in American Football – he played defence for the Hurricanes whilst at Miami University – upon graduation Dwayne was signed to the Calgary Stampeders but a back injury ended all thoughts of progressing through the ranks of Grid Iron. It was then that Johnson turned his thoughts to what was practically a family business: professional wrestling. Dwayne's father was respected heavyweight 'Rocky' Johnson and his grandfather the great Samoan champion Peter Maivia.

With such links to the profession it wasn't hard for Johnson to get the contacts to find work as a wrestler. He made his debut as Flex Kavana and was soon feuding with Jerry 'The King' Lawler for the United States Wrestling Association. By 1996 he had progressed to the WWE, where he was billed as Rocky Maivia. At this time Johnson was a 'heel', incurring the wrath of the fans at ringside for his wicked ways. Over time the 'Rocky' tag was dropped in favour of 'The Rock' and this striking athlete was set for a path of fame that few could have imagined just a few years before. One of his most famous victories came at Wrestlemania X8 when The Rock chalked up a defeat over Hulk Hogan in a thrilling match with wrestling's first superstar. A part in the television series *Star Trek: Voyager* led to his big break in movies playing the Scorpion King in *The Mummy Returns*. Despite further offers from Hollywood and an impressive list of acting appearances, The Rock, a skilled salt water fisherman, has not turned his back on wrestling and continues to feud in the WWE.

DAVE 'FIT' FINLAY

Belfast born Dave Finlay had an outstanding amateur wrestling career with the renowned Carrickfergus Club, Belfast. Having turned professional in 1978 Finlay was forced to move from his native Northern Ireland to mainland Britain in order to gather more experience against world-class wrestlers, and he wasted little time in defeating 'deaf and dumb' campaigner Alan Kilby for the British Heavy-Middleweight belt.

Finlay was regularly escorted to the ring by his flamboyant wife at the time, Princess Paula, ladies' wrestling star Paula Valdez. Her presence at ringside infuriated fans and Finlay's opponents alike. She would often slap her husband around the face if he had conceded a fall and attack his opponents if tempers were high.

A regular globetrotter, Finlay travelled Europe taking on all the local stars in an effort to widen his reputation and knowledge of the sport. His big break came in 1995 when he made his debut for WCW as the 'Belfast Brawler' – Finlay's aggressive style made him perfect for the anything goes American wrestling promotions. Having defeated Chris Benoit to take the Television Title, Finlay's career then hung in the balance when he was thrown through a table by Brian Knobbs, which sliced his leg open. A surgeon operated immediately but only gave Dave a 50 per cent chance of walking again. However, he was not finished yet and battled his way back to fitness – he was after all 'Fit' Finlay – continuing to compete in WCW until their takeover by WWE. Today Finlay works as Road Manager for WWE and still steps into the ring from time to time.

'CRY BABY' JIM BREAKS

Although it is usually the big men of wrestling who get the most attention, Bradford's Jim Breaks is among the élite of lighter stars whose ring antics helped fill halls over two decades. Breaks had been a physical training instructor with the Duke of Wellington's army regiment before turning professional as a wrestler in the 1960s. Although never one to let the rule book stand in the way of a win, Breaks was quick in securing the British Lightweight Championship at the Royal Albert Hall with a victory over Rochdale's Melwyn Riss.

Breaks acquired his nickname by always showing a tendency for childish tantrums when he pushed opponents too far and they retaliated in a no-holds-barred style. Similarly, Jim was never short of a sharp word for opponents, referees or indeed anyone at ringside who caught his attention. This trait never masked the fact that Jim Breaks was a brilliant lightweight wrestler who could compete with the very pinnacle of the fast brigade. Breaks now lives in Gran Canaria, where he has property interests, but he still owns the 'Seconds Out' pub in Wakefield, England.

HULK HOGAN

Globally there can be few bigger names in the wrestling world than Hulk Hogan. Hailing from Venice Beach in California, the young Terry Bollea began his working life touring rock clubs as a guitarist. In the audience one night there were a couple of wrestlers who were immediately taken aback by his 6' 7" muscled frame. They persuaded Terry that he would be a natural in the wrestling ring and he made his debut in 1978 as 'The Super Destroyer'. Initially working for small independent promotions through the United States, he was a modest success. It took Vince McMahon Jr to realise Terry Bollea's true potential when he signed him to the Worldwide Wrestling Federation. This ultimately became the WWE and it was here that 'The Hulk' (named after the popular television series and comic book character) surpassed all expectations.

In 1987 over 80,000 spectators packed the Pontiac Silver Dome to see Hogan victorious over André the Giant, who up to that point had never been defeated. Life got even better for The Hulkster, when in 1989 he earned an incredible $1.8 million for wrestling 'Macho Man' Randy Savage at Wrestlemania V. After such massive success in the WWE, Hulk Hogan shocked the world when he signed for rival promotion WCW in 1994. Under the new banner, Hulk Hogan turned villain and restyled himself into 'Hollywood Hogan', proving just as popular as when he was the hero. When eventually the WCW was bought out by Vince McMahon's WWE it meant that The Hulk had returned to the home of his greatest triumphs.

THE CLOTHES LINE

One of the most celebrated and visually exciting moves in world wrestling is 'The Clothes Line'. This fast-paced manoeuvre is where a combatant is flung across the ring at high speed only for them to bounce off the ropes and return in the direction of their aggressor, who is lying in wait with his arm at full stretch looking to catch the opponent across the upper chest.

BRET 'THE HITMAN' HART

As his motto proclaims, Bret Hart is 'The best there is, the best there was, the best there ever will be…'
– and few who have seen his incredible grapple action would disagree.

Coming from the famous Hart wrestling dynasty of Canada, Bret had the toughest training going courtesy of his father who ran the infamous Dungeon Gym in the basement of the family home. This stood him in good stead, with Bret soon becoming a star performer for his father's organisation, Stampede Promotions. Then WWE owner Vince McMahon came along and bought out Bret's father and a wrestling superstar was born. It is right to say that his wrestling skill and athleticism have earned Bret a unique place in the annals of professional wrestling. Initially appearing as the heel or bad guy, Bret soon turned good and gathered an army of WWE fans devoted to his hard and fast action style.

Despite his amazing popularity with the fans, relations were not good between Bret and WWE boss Vince McMahon, culminating in Bret quitting WWE. It wasn't long before he was back in grapple action though, this time for rival organisation WCW, taking the world title to add to his already impressive array of honours. Vince's and Bret's paths crossed once again when the promoter took over WCW, but on hearing this 'The Hitman' opted to retire rather than work for his former boss.

In 2002 disaster struck when Bret was out on his motorbike, which hit a pothole and caused him to crash land on his head resulting in an instantaneous stroke. With paralysis down one side of his body, the road back to fitness has been long and hard for Bret. He has recently acted on stage but has so far refused several offers to appear at WWE events. Retired from wrestling perhaps, but still the best there is, was or ever will be.

KLONDYKE KATE

Klondyke Kate has become synonymous with ladies wrestling. At 5' 3" tall and weighing 20 stone, Kate (real name Jayne Drosdzowski) more than lives up to her billing as 'Hell In Boots'. As a young girl Kate was a regular at her local wrestling hall in Stoke, and during family holidays to Blackpool would attend promotions at the Horseshoe Showbar, the illustrious north-east England wrestling venue. One night during a bout featuring 'The Mighty Chang', blood splattered all over her dress as she sat at ringside. Furious that her clothing had been ruined she stormed over to promoter Bobby Barron and complained. The conversation turned to Kate's obsession with wrestling and Barron asked if she'd like to do some training with the wrestlers. Kate leapt at the chance and, aged just 14, made her debut in a tag match with Rusty Blair. She would learn much of the business from pioneering British lady wrestler Mitzi Mueller whom she battled regularly until Mitzi's enforced retirement. Kate went from strength to strength, her obvious bulk and talent for winding up the crowds making her a figure the wrestling public loves to hate. Having toured the globe, Kate can claim to be one of the most experienced lady wrestlers in the world. Kate has often thought nothing of taking on the big men in mixed tag matches, and has proved time and again she can hold her own with anyone who dares step into the squared circle with her. Still wrestling, Klondyke Kate has taken a great interest in the future generation of grapplers and often runs training clubs.

MICK MᶜMANUS

He's never had a grey hair on his head. Not one. Rumours have abounded as to the origins of Mick's hair colour but no comment has been made from the one man who really knows. When British television began their coverage of wrestling in 1955, one of the first screen stars of the sport was Mick McManus. With his bulldog-like features and slicked jet black hair he was the archetypal ring villain.

Mick was born on the Old Kent Road, London, and as a teenager showed a keen interest in amateur wrestling. He joined the local John Ruskin Club and battled his way through the amateur leagues before serving with the Royal Air Force. It was during this time that he fought his first match against a professional, Jimmy Rudd, and, having showed such promise in the bout, upon leaving the RAF Mick decided to try wrestling full time and since then has never looked back.

Mick's celebrated forearm smash shook up many an opponent and his natural ring arrogance and tendency for punches blind side of the referee had viewers at home writing to the studios insisting that he be banned from wrestling altogether. 'People might not always like my style and tactics but it has certainly paid dividends time and time again and I am certainly not thinking of changing now.'

Mick held many wrestling championships. He hung up his boots after a match against Catweazle in 1982. A keen collector of antiques, Mick is now recognised as an authority on the subject.

'WILDCAT'
ROBBIE BROOKSIDE

Brookside first became interested in wrestling when his aunt took him to see shows at the now demolished Liverpool Stadium. Despite showing promise at football, he became obsessed with professional wrestling. After training at the Liverpool Olympic Wrestling Club, he found himself at the infamous Horseshoe Showbar, Blackpool, where aged 15 he joined the rota of wrestlers who would challenge the public to last three rounds with them for a cash prize.

This handsome and athletic young man came to the attention of leading promoter Brian Dixon and before long Robbie was touring holiday camps and seaside resorts as a fully fledged professional wrestler. The true launchpad for his career proved to be a regular tag partnership with his fellow Scouse grappler Ian 'Doc' Dean. As 'The Liverpool Lads' they became one of the most in demand tag teams on the British circuit – their long hair and toned physiques making them firm favourites with the ladies.

The pair toured mainland Europe and wrestled a number of bouts in WCW. When Dean went to live in America permanently Robbie continued in solo combat. One of the highlights of Robbie's career, following a sensational night in Croydon, was winning the World Heavy-Middleweight title vacated by Mark 'Rollerball' Rocco.

Robbie Brookside continues to wrestle all over the world and is today considered one of the finest ambassadors for British wrestling.

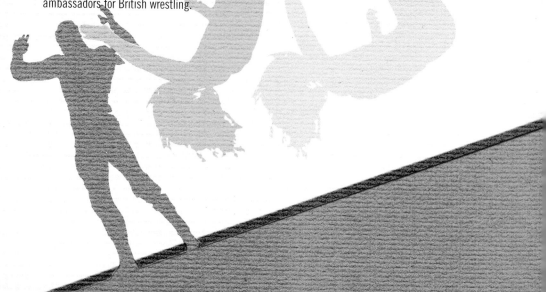

MARK 'ROLLERBALL' ROCCO

The self-proclaimed 'Mean Machine' and 'Master of Disaster' has left behind a legacy among wrestling fans as perhaps one of the most exciting men ever to climb into the ring. As a youngster Mark was a keen equestrian and indeed competed for his country, but the lure of the wrestling ring was in the family blood. Mark's father is the equally legendary matman 'Jumping' Jim Hussey and it was in his father's gym that Mark would meet many wrestlers who would visit to train with Hussey. 'My father banned me from the gym' Mark reflects. 'He had poured his life savings into providing me with the finest showjumping equipment and horses. Unbeknown to him though, when he was away wrestling, the members of his gym were teaching me all the moves and giving me a good grounding in the sport.'

From the start it was obvious that Rocco's energy and aggression would make big waves on the UK grappling circuit. Mark became a huge star in international rings too, particularly in Japan where he was known as 'Black Tiger', and his matches with the likes of the original 'Tiger Mask' and 'Dynamite Kid' in the land of the rising sun have passed into wrestling folklore. 'I was told that my match with "Tiger Mask" had the biggest TV wrestling audience ever in Japan. This was because they had played a primetime cartoon of our characters for six months before the match, which made the actual clash a sensation.'

'Rollerball' rates his best matches to be those against Marty Jones and 'Dynamite Kid'. Among the many titles he won was the World Heavy-Middleweight Championship with a victory at a packed Madison Square Garden. However, his 22-year career in the ring ended prematurely when it was discovered that Mark was suffering from a heart condition that forced him to give up the World Heavy-Middleweight title and retire from the sport. 'The characters I worked with were all larger than life. Only in wrestling could you meet such personalities with each and every one a true gentleman. 'I wouldn't have missed it for the world.'

THE PILE DRIVER

'The Pile Driver' is not only a technically difficult move to master but also requires an extreme display of physical strength. Usually started from a standing position, the opponent's head is trapped between the aggressor's knees, then, in a swift motion, the aggressor drops to the ground, stunning his opponent. A spectacular move that is only dared to be attempted by wrestling's true élite.

'MACHO MAN' RANDY SAVAGE

The vibrant 'Macho Man' has long been one of wrestling's most outlandish and colourful characters. Real name Randy Poffo, he had some success as a baseball player before his father, wrestler Angelo Poffo, enticed him into the squared circle. One of Randy's earliest gimmicks was as a masked wrestler called 'The Spider'. However this was short-lived and he joined his brother Lanny in wrestling for their father's own promotion International Championship Wrestling. During this time Randy showed little brotherly love, defeating his sibling for the ICW World Heavyweight title. Randy changed his ring name and image not long after on account of fellow wrestler Ole Anderson commenting that he wrestled like a savage and from then on it was a very different character who stepped out of the dressing room.

By 1985 Randy wound up in the WWE and would go on to participate in one of the greatest ever WWE match ups when at Wrestlemania III he took on the giant Ricky 'The Dragon' Steamboat in a thrill-a-second pairing.

Savage was often accompanied to bouts by his then wife 'Miss Elizabeth', and opponents would try and get at the 'Macho Man' through her, provoking some truly amazing storylines. Possibly as a result of such antics he later parted with Elizabeth, although he wasn't found to be short of company as he was soon seen being escorted to the ring by several equally beautiful ladies. Since retiring from the grapple game Randy Savage has been in the blockbuster movie *Spiderman* and has also released a rap CD – 'Be a Man' – a career event that he got a bigger battering from than any wrestling match!

'MIGHTY' JOHN QUINN

Former Canadian lumberjack John Quinn became one of the biggest box office stars of the 1970s and 1980s in the UK when on national television he branded the British 'cowards' and threw out a challenge to all heavyweights to step in the ring with him. One quick to accept was Big Daddy and their feud would climax in a sold-out clash at Wembley Arena before 10,000 people.

Standing 6' 5'' tall the man mountain from British Columbia had been a stalwart of Stu Hart's Stampede Promotion as well as following the tournament circuit in Europe, where he was always placed highly in such competitions as the 'World Cup' in Hanover. Quinn caused a major upset in 1980 when he defeated Wayne Bridges to hold the World Heavyweight title, with Bridges having to retire from the match due to a bad wound on the forehead inflicted by the Canadian giant. Regularly tagging with the likes of Yasu Fuji, Giant Haystacks and Kendo Nagasaki, John Quinn can be counted as one of the most successful ever imports from foreign shores for British promoters. After retiring from wrestling, Quinn moved back to his native Canada and for a while was involved in the hotel and restaurant trade. Following a period of ill health John Quinn is well on the road to recovery and is regarded as one of the greatest 'heel' heavyweights of all time.

YOKOZUNA

The sumo wrestling styled Yokozuna rates as one of the heaviest ever participants on the professional wrestling circuit, standing 6' 4" in height, and tipping the scales at a whopping 42 stone. Starting his career in Japan, Rodney Anaoi debuted in wrestling as Kokina Maximus for the AWA before entering the WWE. Although Anaoi came from Polynesia, he was billed as Japanese and given the name Yokozuna, which is the highest level that can be achieved in sumo wrestling.

Yokozuna literally squashed his opponents, his devastating 'Bonzai Drop' would shake the foundations of buildings across the globe. During one stunt for the WWE, Yokozuna's manager Mr Fuji challenged anybody to pick up and slam Yokozuna on the deck of the USS *Intrepid* aircraft carrier in New York City. Many tried and failed until a helicopter landed and out stormed professional wrestler Lex Lugar who successfully picked up and slammed to the canvas the mighty Yokozuna in an amazing show of physical strength. Throughout his career Yokozuna was encouraged to lose weight as it was seen as a major health problem. The crunch came in the mid-1990s when he failed a medical set by the New York State Athletic Commission which revoked his licence to wrestle in many US states. Not to be deterred, Yokozuna subsequently found work on the independent circuit and overseas. However, whilst on tour in the UK during 2000, Rodney was found dead in his hotel room in Liverpool, apparently having suffered a fatal heart attack aged just 33.

CATWEAZLE

If your name was Gary Cooper you might be forgiven if expectations proved to be a little high. The famous film star's namesake is better known to wrestling fans as 'Catweazle'. The original *Catweazle* was a creation for children's television, the story of a medieval vagabond who found himself swept through time to the modern day. Doncaster-based Gary Cooper's facial features were so similar to that of the television character that out went Gary and in came Catweazle.

Always entering the hall in his familiar sackcloth, Catweazle proved time and again that he was among wrestling's finest jesters. Having a plastic frog in his corner for good luck, Cooper's lanky figure in a striped Edwardian bathing costume was enough to put a smile on the sternest face. It was not unknown for his dentures to fly across the ring during bouts, invariably reducing everyone including opponents and the referee to uncontrollable laughter. Despite his comic appearance Catweazle was a formidable opponent and came away with victories over many top wrestlers of the day. Catweazle died in 1993, robbing professional wrestling of one of its most memorable characters.

THE UNDERTAKER

When the familiar 'bong' of a bell tolls in a darkened arena, fans worldwide know that the arrival of The Undertaker will surely follow. The infamous 'Dead Man' has been at the heart of WWE's promotions for 15 years and shows no sign of letting up.

Mark Calloway from Houston, Texas, used his 6' 8" stature to great advantage in basketball, but it wasn't long before he discovered wrestling as a way of making every inch count in his favour. Calloway had his first professional contest in 1988 as the masked 'Texas Red', his opponent being the feared 'Bruiser' Brody who more than lived up to his name when tackling the rookie. Gaining some experience on the independent wrestling circuit the more familiar guise of The Undertaker made his first appearance in 1990. A year later The Undertaker caused a major upset by defeating the seemingly invincible Hulk Hogan for the WWE title and his entry into the all-time greats was secured. Calloway's athleticism during his matches continued to astound onlookers, with a speed and agility rarely found in such a big man. For a while Calloway transformed his character into a Harley Davidson-riding leather-clad biker, but more recently he has once again donned the black garb of the macabre man from the dark side, reviving his original image. The Undertaker truly stands as one of the iconic images of world wrestling, long may he wrestle in peace.

GIANT HAYSTACKS

Standing 6' 11" tall and weighing in excess of 46 stones at his peak, Giant Haystacks earned himself an entry into the *Guinness Book of World Records* as the World's Heaviest Sportsman.

This huge man had been working in construction and as a nightclub bouncer before being spotted by local wrestler Billy Graham. Graham knew immediately that his immense size would be an attraction in the wrestling ring, so Haystacks was trained and persuaded to make his debut at a private function as the opponent of 'The Mighty Chang' – the bout quickly turned into all-out brawling, resulting in both men being disqualified.

Anxious to learn more Haystacks accepted an offer from India and grapple fans there were suitably impressed. Haystacks soon stood opposite the great Indian champion Dara Singh. The mammoth ring monster proved to be box office gold and when he eventually returned to his native Salford, Manchester, England, promoters were eager to sign the impressive newcomer whose reputation had quickly become known through the wrestling grapevine. With Big Daddy as his tag partner, the biggest tag team Britain had ever produced flattened all of the opposition and even bigger crowds gathered when the two former partners turned on each other and began a feud that would define the crowd-pulling ability of the sport. 'Don't bring me midgets, bring men' became Haystacks' battle cry after he had literally squashed yet another opponent.

In 1980 Haystacks set out on an extended world tour which would see him squaring up to no less than the great André the Giant – a truly awesome sight. Travelling the world did however come with a downside, with international air travel being a source of discomfort particularly on one trip to India. 'I had to go to the loo when the light flashed on for landing', Haystacks recalled. 'I tried to leave but couldn't – I was wedged tight. There was nothing anybody could do. So the plane landed and firemen had to hack out a door at the back of the toilet to release me.'

Haystacks wrestled under many pseudonyms overseas including 'Luke McMasters', 'Goliath' and 'The Loch Ness Monster' although his real name was Martin Ruane. In 1996 Ted Turner's World Championship Wrestling (WCW) signed Haystacks for an extended contract in the USA, where it was planned that he would eventually be Hulk Hogan's tag partner. However, during a routine trip home Haystacks collapsed and was rushed to hospital where he was diagnosed as suffering from cancer. Despite intensive chemotherapy this genial man, so different from his ring persona, passed away in 1998, aged just 52.

ANDRÉ THE GIANT

Standing 7' 2" tall and weighing over 500 pounds, André the Giant's billing as 'the Eighth Wonder of the World' was never in dispute. Born Jean Ferre Roussimoff in Grenoble in the French Alps during 1946, it was soon clear that there was something quite extraordinary about the man who would come to be known as André. Suffering from acromegaly or 'gigantism', he would stand 6' 7" by the time he was 17. A man of such proportions was easily noticed and it wasn't long before French wrestling promoters came to hear of the man mountain walking the streets.

Revelling in such ring aliases as 'Monster Eiffel Tower' he eventually came to the attention of Canadian wrestler Edouard Carpentier. Carpentier could see many opportunities for the mighty Frenchman in the USA, and after approaching André with his plan he quickly contacted promoters in the States. In the meantime André toured the UK and the rest of mainland Europe gaining experience which would stand him in good stead for his time in America. He made a memorable debut at the Royal Albert Hall, London, in the late 1960s, striding into the arena and entering the ring by simply stepping over the top rope!

When in 1972 Vince McMahon Snr signed André to his flourishing WWWF promotion, a box office sensation was born. From then on André's name on a bill could pack venues such as Madison Square Garden as people flocked to see the Eighth Wonder taking on all comers. It was inevitable that a man André's size would capture the attention of showbusiness moguls and he made his acting debut with two acclaimed episodes of *The Six Million Dollar Man* playing the mythical Big Foot. He would also have guest roles in *BJ and the Bear*, *The Fall Guy* and in the movies *Conan the Destroyer* and *The Princess Bride*, which was André's personal favourite.

Always a quietly spoken and gentle individual outside the ring, André's ability to drink enough alcohol to kill lesser men during a night out became the stuff of legend. Sadly the effects of his condition caused his health to deteriorate, he could no longer wrestle and took to walking with a stick. During a trip home to attend his father's funeral in 1993, André was found dead in his hotel room a few days after apparently having suffered a heart attack. Wrestlers and fans around the globe mourned the loss of the gentle giant who had made such an impact on everyone who met him or saw his greatness in the ring.

THE ULTIMATE WARRIOR™

The wild hair and jagged face make-up would make The Ultimate Warrior one of the biggest stars in wrestling during the 1980s and 1990s. The Warrior started out as Jim Helwig, a body builder and keep fit fanatic. He was studying in Atlanta to be a chiropractor whilst entering such prestigious competitions as Mr America. Through his bodybuilding contacts he met Steve Borden, otherwise known to wrestling fans as 'Sting', and together they formed a tag alliance known as 'The Bladerunners'. When the tag partnership broke up Helwig headed to the Dallas Promotion run by Fritz Von Erich where he wrestled as 'The Dingo Warrior'. This gimmick was the first stage in a persona that would capture the imagination of wrestling fans all over the world.

When Dingo Warrior arrived in WWE, big things were afoot and the change of name to The Ultimate Warrior saw the rise to headline status. The pinnacle of the Warrior's career saw him defeating the immortal Hulk Hogan for the heavyweight title. Jim Helwig became so entrenched in the character that he legally changed his name to Warrior. A long and bitter battle ensued with Vince McMahon for the right to use the Warrior persona in wrestling rings, and despite a brief return to WWE in 1996, the animosity between Warrior and Vince McMahon led to him being released from his contract.

Having won his courtroom battle to use his ring persona, Warrior was next seen in WCW battling his old adversary Hogan and, ironically, was paired with his very first tag partner Sting for a series of epic battles. Rumours of his increasingly difficult attitude behind the scenes eventually led to his retirement from the wrestling scene. The Warrior has since built himself a mail order empire based around his character and philosophy which includes comic books, gyms and health advice. More recently the wrestling icon has been touring colleges teaching students his ideology for success on a personal and professional path.

A wrestler can gain incredible speed by rebounding himself off the ring ropes – and with such momentum an opponent cannot fail but be toppled into a winning fall by 'The Flying Press'.

THE FLYING PRESS

PAT 'BOMBER' ROACH

Pat, a powerful man at 6' 4" tall and some 19 stone, started earning money at fairgrounds taking on all comers in the wrestling and boxing booths. Having trained with Alf Kent in professional wrestling, Pat toured the world, once appearing before 100,000 people wrestling Indian champion Dara Singh. His speciality move was known as the 'Brummagem Bump', where Pat held an opponent above his head and dropped him face first onto the ring canvas.

Pat Roach is recognised as much for his acting as his wrestling. The Birmingham-based strongman is best known as Brian 'Bomber' Busbridge in the comedy-drama *Auf Wiedersehen, Pet,* which ran for four series. Bomber was also seen in Stanley Kubrick's *A Clockwork Orange*, with Sean Connery in the 007 James Bond thriller *Never Say Never Again* and in Steven Spielberg's *Raiders of the Lost Ark.* Despite his popularity with movie producers Pat remained true to his roots, opening the Pat Roach Health Centre in his native Birmingham and continuing with a wrestling schedule that would include regular tussles with Giant Haystacks and other big names in the sport. A final, follow-up episode of *Auf Wiedersehen, Pet* was planned but Pat who had been suffering from health problems was not able to travel to Thailand for the filming. Pat passed away in 2004, aged 67.

'EXOTIC' ADRIAN STREET

A pioneering British wrestler, Adrian Street took glitter, glam and face make-up to extremes and in so doing paved a path to the otherside of the Atlantic. Born in Wales, the young Street couldn't wait to escape the provincial backwaters of his native country and aged 16 headed to London. He found jobs at Wembley Stadium and digging holes for utility companies, but at that time his real passion was bodybuilding. Street already had a formidable physique and earned extra money by boxing in a fairground booth, sometimes several times a day. Street then turned his attention to wrestling and made his debut as 'Kid Tarzan' Jonathan, a name heavily influenced by a favourite American star of the 1960s, Mormon heavyweight Don Leo Jonathan.

Under new management and now billed under his real name as 'Nature Boy' Adrian Street, the aspiring Welsh wrestler took a long hard look at his ring image. Deciding that he needed to make his way to main event status, his hair was bleached blond and colourful grapple outfits commissioned. Soon the wolf whistles were flying, and as the Glam Rock phenomenon swept over the British music scene, Street adopted similar outlandish face make-up – he was pretty much a drag queen in wrestling boots. Together with 'Bad Boy' Bobby Barnes they became 'The Hells Angels' tag team, whipping up a storm wherever they appeared.

As the 1980s dawned Adrian and 'Miss Linda' – Adrian's wrestle star wife – left the UK for new challenges, which took them to Canada, Germany, Mexico and eventually the USA. Street played the Americans at their own game, his own 'Exotic' image outshining all those he got in the ring with, and before long feuds were going on with all the major players including 'Macho Man' Randy Savage. Like many before and since, Street eventually turned his thoughts to the training of future stars at his 'Skullkrushers' gym, coupling this with his 'Bizarre Bazaar', a boutique supplying outfits and equipment to the industry. After a battle with throat cancer, Adrian is taking things a little more sedately at his Florida base. He and Linda are still 'Exotic' but perhaps a little less energetic.

INDEX

First published in Great Britain in 2005 by Weidenfeld & Nicolson

Text © Rob Cope & Kendo Nagasaki 2005
Design and layout copyright © Weidenfeld & Nicolson 2005

A CIP catalogue record for this book is available from the British Library.

ISBN 0 297 84419 9

With the exception of the following all photographs are courtesy of Russell Plummer:

2005 George Napolitano by CMG Worldwide, Inc. www.CMGWorldwide.com: 17, 21, 27, 40–41, 58, 59, 69, 71, 72, 76; Action Images / MSI: 22, 22 (top) , 23 (inset), 65; Action Plus: 4, 30, 31, 62; Corbis: 26, 37, 38, 39; Getty Images: 36, 42, 54; ITV/LWT: 7; Kendo Nagasaki: 8–9, 10, 12–13, 15.

The Grapple Manual

In memory of Mark Cope (1968–1985) and Martin Ruane (1946–1998)

The author and publishers wish to thank and acknowledge the many people who have generously given their time and knowledge during the creation of this book: Brian Dixon of All Star Wrestling, Russell Plummer for his comprehensive collection of photographs, Robbie Brookside, Jeff Wilde, Paul Hussey, David Fleming at Kendonagasaki.com, Johnny Saint, 'Main Man' Marty Jones, 'Mighty' John Quinn, Tony St Clair, Klondyke Kate, Paul Douglas at British Wrestling Legends, Ian Wilshaw, Simon 'Bone-crusher' Bond, Howard Cope, Lawrence Stevens, Lloyd Ryan, Mal Mason, Frank Rimer and Josh Smith.

The legends featured in this book are just a small selection of the hundreds of wrestlers who have graced our television screens and wrestling halls over the years. There are so many more we could have featured. Truly great grapplers such as 'King Kong' Kirk, Tony St Clair, Johnny Saint, Triple H, William Regal, 'Stone Cold' Steve Austin, Shawn Michaels, Jackie 'Mr TV' Pallo, Leon Arras, Wayne Bridges, Dara Singh, Les Kellett, Vic Faulkner, Johnny Kwango, Mike Marino, Bert Royal, Bobby Barnes, Jimmy Savile and Tibor Szakacs – the list is endless. We hope though to beg your forgiveness for narrowing down to the featured action heroes. It would have taken a volume the size of the *Encyclopaedia Britannica* to include them all. Suffice to say, all of them are worthy of inclusion. Maybe next time…

Introduction by Kendo Nagasaki
Foreword by Dickie Davies
Text by Rob Cope
Copy-edited by Claire Wedderburn-Maxwell
Index by Mike Solomons
Addtional illustrations by N. Duncan Mills
Designed by DR. Ink, info@d-r-ink.com
Created & edited by Matt Lowing

For information on getting involved in the colourful
world of professional wrestling visit www.dropkixx.com